Benjamin Franklin

by Lucia Raatma

Compass Point Early Biographies

Content Adviser: Professor Sherry L. Field,
Department of Social Science Education, College of Education,
The University of Georgia

Reading Adviser: Dr. Linda D. Labbo,
Department of Reading Education, College of Education,
The University of Georgia

COMPASS POINT BOOKS

Minneapolis, Minnesota

Compass Point Books
3722 West 50th Street, #115
Minneapolis, MN 55410

Visit Compass Point Books on the Internet at *www.compasspointbooks.com* or e-mail your
request to *custserv@compasspointbooks.com*

Editors: E. Russell Primm and Emily J. Dolbear
Photo Researcher: Svetlana Zhurkina
Photo Selector: Linda S. Koutris
Designer: Bradfordesign, Inc.

Library of Congress Cataloging-in-Publication Data

Raatma, Lucia.
    Benjamin Franklin / by Lucia Raatma.
        p. cm. — (Compass Point early biographies)
    Includes bibliographical references and index.
    ISBN 0-7565-0067-2
            1. Franklin, Benjamin, 1706–1790—Juvenile literature. 2. Statesmen—United States—
Biography—Juvenile literature. 3. Printers—United States—Biography—Juvenile literature.
4. Inventors—United States—Biography—Juvenile literature. [1. Franklin, Benjamin, 1706–1790.
2. Statesmen. 3. Inventors.] I. Title. II. Series.
    E302.6.F8 R12 2001
    973.3'092—dc21   00-010937

Table of Contents

An Important Person

Benjamin Franklin was a very important person in U.S. history. He was one of the Founding Fathers of the United States. The Founding Fathers were a group of men who helped make the thirteen colonies into a new country.

We remember Benjamin Franklin for many things. We remember Benjamin Franklin as a scientist. We remember him as an **inventor**. We also remember him as a **statesman**. A statesman is a person skilled in government business.

◀ Benjamin Franklin was a scientist, an inventor, and a statesman.

Benjamin Franklin was such an important person in U.S. history that his picture appears on every $100 bill.

Young Benjamin

Benjamin Franklin was born on January 17, 1706, in Boston, Massachusetts. He had sixteen brothers and sisters.

Benjamin Franklin's birthplace

Benjamin's family was not rich. Everyone in the family worked hard. His father made and sold candles and soap in his own shop.

◀ A picture of Benjamin Franklin on the U.S. $100 bill

Benjamin worked with his father
making candles and soap.

Young Benjamin started school when he was eight. When he was ten, he left school to work in his father's shop.

Then he worked for his brother James. James had a printing press. Benjamin learned all he could about the printing business. And in his free time he read books.

Working for a Newspaper

When Benjamin was fifteen, James started a newspaper called the *New England Courant*. During the day, Benjamin delivered the newspaper. At night, he wrote articles for it. He wrote about life as a **colonist** living in Massachusetts.

Benjamin learned all he could about printing and printing presses.

During this time, America was not yet a country. It was a group of thirteen colonies that were governed by Britain. Benjamin complained about Britain in some of his newspaper articles. Those articles made the leaders of Britain angry.

THE
New-England Courant.

[Nº 58

From MONDAY September 3. to MONDAY September 10. 1722.

Quod est in corde sobrii, est in ore ebrii.

To the Author of the New-England Courant.

SIR,

[No XII.

T is no unprofitable tho' unpleasant Pursuit, diligently to inspect and consider the Manners & Conversation of Men, who, insensible of the greatest Enjoyments of humane Life, abandon themselves to Vice from a false Notion of *Pleasure* and *good Fellowship*. A true and natural Representation of any Enormity, is often the best Argument against it and Means of removing it, when the most severe Reprehensions alone, are found ineffectual.

I WOULD in this Letter improve the little Observation I have made on the Vice of *Drunkenness*, the Devotions of the Evening to *Bacchus*.

I DOUBT not but *moderate Drinking* has been improv'd for the Diffusion of Knowledge among the ingenious Part of Mankind, who want the Talent

led Appetite. What Pleasure can the Drunkard have in the Reflection, that, while in his Cups, he retain'd only the Shape of a Man, and acted the Part of a Beast; or that from reasonable Discourse a few Minutes before, he descended to Impertinence and Nonsense?

I CANNOT pretend to account for the different Effects of Liquor on Persons of different Dispositions, who are guilty of Excess in the Use of it. 'Tis strange to see Men of a regular Conversation become rakish and profane when intoxicated with Drink, and yet more surprizing to observe, that some who appear to be the most profligate Wretches when sober, become mighty religious in their Cups, and will then, and at no other Time address their Maker, but when they are destitute of Reason, and actually affronting him. Some shrink in the Wetting, and others swell to such an unusual Bulk in their Imaginations, that they can in an Instant understand all Arts and Sciences, by the liberal Education of a little vivifying *Punch*, or a sufficient Quantity of other exhilerating Liquor.

AND as the Effects of Liquor are various, so are some Shame in the Drunkards themselves, in that they have invented numberless Words and Phrases to cover their Folly, whose proper Sgnifications are harmless, or have no Signification at all. They are

Leaving Boston

Benjamin moved to Philadelphia, Pennsylvania, when he was seventeen. There he made friends with an Englishman in charge of Pennsylvania. His name was Sir William Keith.

Sir William Keith, one of Benjamin Franklin's friends

Keith thought that Benjamin could learn more about printing in England. He told the young man to go to London to work as a printer.

◄ Benjamin delivered and wrote for the *New England Courant*.

One of the printers Benjamin Franklin worked for in London

So, at age eighteen, Benjamin Franklin traveled to London. He worked for two important printing offices there.

Young Benjamin worked hard in London and many people began to admire him. He wrote and spoke well. Benjamin was also very responsible and a good leader.

Life in Philadelphia

Two years later, Benjamin Franklin returned to Philadelphia. He bought a newspaper called the *Pennsylvania Gazette*. The newspaper had been badly written. It was not very successful.

Soon, Benjamin improved the paper. People enjoyed his wisdom. They also liked his sense of humor. Benjamin's newspaper became a success.

A front page of the *Pennsylvania Gazette*

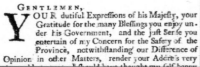

In 1730, when he was twenty-four years old, Benjamin Franklin got married. His wife's name was Deborah Read. She was also from Philadelphia.

In time, Benjamin Franklin made a name for himself in Philadelphia. He started the first public library in the colonies. He also worked as a **clerk** for the Pennsylvania General Assembly.

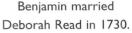

Benjamin married Deborah Read in 1730.

Benjamin Franklin started the first public library in America.

When he was twenty-six, Benjamin wrote a book called *Poor Richard's Almanack*. It was full of advice, jokes, and down-to-earth ideas. It also gave weather forecasts.

Benjamin wrote this book under a different name— Richard Saunders. People loved it, so he wrote a new *Almanack* every year.

A picture from *Poor Richard's Almanack*

Inventor and Scientist

Throughout his life, Benjamin Franklin was interested in science. He experimented and invented new things. One thing he invented was the Franklin stove. It gave off more heat than other stoves and used much less fuel.

During his travels across the Atlantic Ocean, Benjamin studied water currents. He thought of ways to improve ships.

Benjamin Franklin invented many things, including this heating stove.

Benjamin Franklin learned about electricity by flying a kite in a thunderstorm.

Benjamin Franklin experimented with electricity. During a storm, he used a kite to fly a metal key high up in the sky. He wondered what would happen when lightning hit the key.

Benjamin discovered that lightning is electricity. His experiments led to the invention of the lightning rod. Lightning rods protect buildings from lightning.

A lightning rod protects buildings during thunderstorms.

17

Another famous invention was the result of Benjamin Franklin's bad eyesight. He had two pairs of glasses. He used one pair for reading. The other pair helped him see things that were far away.

Because Benjamin had poor eyesight, he invented special glasses to help him see better.

Benjamin Franklin cut the glasses in half and combined them. With only one pair of glasses, he could see both up close and far away. These glasses were called **bifocals**. Many people wear bifocals today.

Working for the People

When he was forty-two, Benjamin Franklin sold his printing press. He began to work in other areas. He was elected to the Pennsylvania General Assembly. He also worked as postmaster for all the colonies.

Benjamin Franklin was a member of the Pennsylvania General Assembly.

Possession of the Publishers.

In time, more colonists grew angry about being ruled by Britain. In many ways, Benjamin Franklin liked Britain. He wanted to help work out the problems.

In 1757, at age fifty-one, he went to Britain. He met with the king. He talked about the problems in the colonies. Benjamin Franklin represented the American colonies in Britain for five years.

While in Britain, Benjamin Franklin spoke in the House of Commons.

Colonists dressed as Indians dumped tea ➤ into Boston Harbor because they were angry about taxes.

The colonists were most unhappy about taxes. British taxes made things in the colonies cost more. The colonists did not think this was

The Battle of Bunker Hill was the bloodiest battle in the American Revolution.

fair. If they had to pay taxes, they wanted to have a voice in the British government.

Benjamin Franklin worked hard to keep Britain from adding new taxes. But he was not successful. The colonists grew angrier.

When Benjamin returned to the colonies in 1775, the American Revolution had already started. The colonies had decided they didn't want to be ruled by Britain. They wanted to run their own country.

During the American Revolution, Benjamin Franklin had many important roles. He helped write the Declaration of Independence. He was one of the signers too. This **document** said that the colonies were free of Britain.

Benjamin Franklin also won support for the war from the French. He traveled to France many times. The French people liked Benjamin Franklin.

Benjamin Franklin helped write the Declaration of Independence.

Benjamin Franklin lived in France for many years after the war.

After the American colonies won their independence, Benjamin Franklin worked on the peace agreement with Britain. Then he lived in France for many years. He helped France change its government.

Back in Philadelphia

In 1785, Benjamin Franklin returned to Philadelphia. There he helped write the U.S. Constitution. This document said what kind of country the United States wanted to be.

Benjamin Franklin also worked to end slavery in the United States. Sadly, he was not successful. Slavery was a problem for many years to come.

Benjamin Franklin helped write the U.S. Constitution.

On April 17, 1790, Benjamin Franklin died in his home in Philadelphia. He was eighty-four years old.

People remember Benjamin Franklin for his ability to talk to people. People remember his curious mind and sense of humor. And people respect him for working to make the United States a new country.

Benjamin Franklin's grave site ➤
in Philadelphia, Pennsylvania

Important Dates in Benjamin Franklin's Life

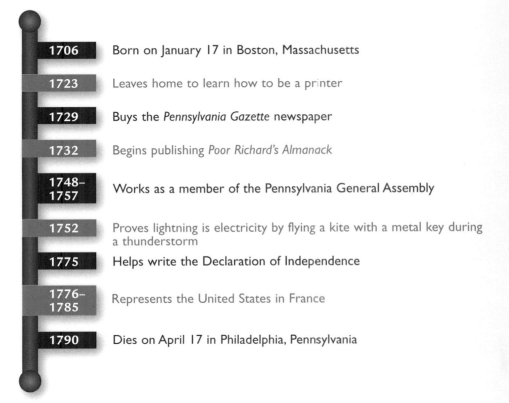

1706 — Born on January 17 in Boston, Massachusetts

1723 — Leaves home to learn how to be a printer

1729 — Buys the *Pennsylvania Gazette* newspaper

1732 — Begins publishing *Poor Richard's Almanack*

1748–1757 — Works as a member of the Pennsylvania General Assembly

1752 — Proves lightning is electricity by flying a kite with a metal key during a thunderstorm

1775 — Helps write the Declaration of Independence

1776–1785 — Represents the United States in France

1790 — Dies on April 17 in Philadelphia, Pennsylvania

28

Glossary

bifocals—a pair of glasses with two lenses—one for seeing up close and one for seeing farther away

clerk—a person who keeps records in a local or state government

colonist—a person who lives in a newly settled area

document—a paper that contains important information

inventor—a person who produces something useful for the first time

statesman—a person skilled in government business

Did You Know?

- Two U.S. presidents had Benjamin Franklin's name: Franklin Pierce and Franklin D. Roosevelt.

- Benjamin Franklin studied five languages, including Latin and Spanish.

- Benjamin Franklin helped create the first university in Pennsylvania and the first city hospital in America.

- In 1763, Benjamin Franklin invented a musical instrument called the glass harmonica.

Want to Know More?

At the Library

Adler, David A. *A Picture Book of Benjamin Franklin*. New York: Holiday House, 1990.

Fleming, Candace. *The Hatmaker's Sign: A Story by Benjamin Franklin*. New York: Orchard Books, 1998.

Scarf, Maggi. *Meet Benjamin Franklin*. New York: Random House, 1989.

On the Web

The Autobiography of Benjamin Franklin

http://www.earlyamerica.com/lives/franklin/index.htm

For fourteen chapters written by Benjamin Franklin about his life

Through the Mail

Independence National Historic Park

313 Walnut Street

Philadelphia, PA 19106

For information about historic sites in Philadelphia related to Benjamin Franklin

On the Road

Benjamin Franklin National Memorial

The Franklin Institute Science Museum

222 North 20th Street

Philadelphia, PA 19103

215/448-1200

To see a 20-foot (6-meter) tall statue of Benjamin Franklin

Index

About the Author

Lucia Raatma received her bachelor's degree in English literature from the University of South Carolina and her master's degree in cinema studies from New York University. She has written a wide range of books for young people. When she is not researching or writing, she enjoys going to movies, playing tennis, and spending time with her husband, daughter, and golden retriever.